the
witch
doesn't
burn
in
this
one

the
witch
doesn't
burn
in
this
one

amanda lovelace

Andrews McMeel
PUBLISHING®

the
women are some kind of magic
series:

the princess saves herself in this one (#1)
the witch doesn't burn in this one (#2)

for the girl on fire.
thank you for inspiring me to
gently set the world alight.
you may have
a gown of flames,
but those same flames
run through my
veins.

&

to all the
princesses,

to all the
damsels,

to all the
queens.

you have
rescued yourselves

so many
times now

& i am
in awe of

you.

trigger warning

this book
contains
sensitive material
relating to:

child abuse,
intimate partner abuse,
sexual assault,
eating disorders,
trauma,
death,
murder,
violence,
fire,
menstruation,
transphobia,
& more.

remember
to practice self-care
before, during, & after
reading.

contents

warning I:

this is not
a ~~fairy~~ witch tale.

there are no
witches.

there is no
witch hunt.

there are no
match-boys.

there are no
burnings.

there is no
fiery revolution.

this is simply
a story

where women
fight against

the manmade
structure

that has long
overstayed

its welcome.

warning II:

no mercy
ahead.

"write your fears."

that's what they
told me.

so i picked that
pen up again

& i traced my way
over these

openclosedopen
wounds

until the inky map
led me right to

the very ones who
started it.

then i took
a deep breath

& conjured up
a storm

all my own.

tell me
something,
would you?

haven't you
ever wished

you could
dance

in the ashes
of everyone who

ever doubted
your worth

& scoffed at
your words?

(shhh,
it's okay.
i won't tell.)

prophecy I

i will not survive this winter. the boys
with fistfuls of matchsticks are

poundpoundpounding at my
cottage door. while witches

may be flammable, the match-boys
cannot take the heart shape my

lover's lips take when she whispers my
name through the dark. the match-boys

cannot take the mother-to-daughter
tales that will slide off the angry

tongues of my descendants for
centuries to come. the match-boys

cannot take the wronged woman's
wrath of artemis, goddess of

hunt(ing the ones who come for women
like me with hate-filled eyes). i may

not survive the match-boys, but my
bitch-fire will survive them all.

prophecy II

what happens
when you
throw
your match,

> but the
> pastor-preyed witch
> simply refuses to
> catch?

what happens
when you
throw
your stone,

> but the
> adultery-accused wife
> simply refuses to
> bleed?

what happens
when you
throw
your fist (again),

> but your
> truth-talking girlfriend
> simply refuses to
> bruise?

over the span
of centuries
animals evolve to
survive their surroundings,

so
what happens
when women
finally

learn
to
throw
back?

(this.)
(this.)
(this.)
(this.)

& so the tale goes . . .

I. the trial

the boys who spend all their days finger-fiddling with matchsticks line us up & proceed to stick tiny yellow & black truth-telling flowers between our teeth. one by one, they ask us if we know what crime we're guilty of. after a brief pause to gather our thoughts, we say, "the only thing we're guilty of is being women." this is simultaneously the right & wrong answer. to the match-boys, our existence is the darkest form of magic, usually punishable by death.

they don't even know what's coming. how cute.

we shouldn't be afraid of them.

no no no.

they should be afraid of *us*.

- the first lesson in fire.

we give power
to anything we
fancy,

but we may also
take it away
again.

                    just.
                    like.
                    that.

the choice
is entirely
ours

& they
just want to
end us

before we have
the chance to
end them.

- the best kept secret.

i'm afraid
i must confess

i inherited
my mother's rage

& the
mother-rage

that came
before her

& all the
mother-rage

that raced down
every branch

of our tangled up
family tree.

- *nothing can extinguish me.*

to
everyone
who said
my
great-grandmother
had a
wee bit of witch
in her:

she's
got nothing
on me.

- & i've only just begun.

the ground—
it ignites
wherever
a woman's
foot
comes down

& if
you're not
careful,

the
very same
thing
could
happen
to you.

- *some destruction is beautiful.*

this is
an overdue
love letter
to each
& every
woman
who walked
these fields
before me
&
made
the path
soft enough
for me to
walk through
to get to
the side
they could
never reach.

for that,
i owe you
so much.

- but i owe some things to myself, too.

there exists
a fine line

between
being
                    selfish
&
being
                    selfless

&
most days

i can't tell
which side

it is that
i'm on.

&
most days?

i don't
care.

- there are some things i just have to do for me.

why yes,

i am
the girl
with the
arsonist heart
all your fathers
warned you
about

&

once
one tree
catches,
it's not long
before
the whole
forest

lights up.

- *yet i never seem to care who gets hurt.*

gods, i hope i terrify you.

keep
an eye out

for
all those

quietly
reckless,

knotty-haired
girls.

you know
you can't

hold back
a wildfire,

don't you?

- *trouble trouble.*

women:
we can
spin
gold
out of
dirt.

- *bewitching.*

24

women:
we can
magic
              f i r e
out of
              a i r.

- *bewitching II.*

sometimes
women bleed;

sometimes
we do not.

we
cannot be

so easily
divided up

into boxes
wrapped in

pre-packaged
pink lace & ribbons.

- *every woman is authentic.*

women are
considered to be

possessions
before we are ever

considered to be
human beings,

& if our doors
& our windows

are ever smashed in
by wicked men,

then we are deemed
worthless—

foreclosed.
never sold.

so we move out of
our neighborhoods

& we make sister-homes
out of each other.

- *we lock those doors & eat those keys.*

women
learn
to sense
~~what~~ who
danger
looks like
just
by catching
another
woman's eye
from across
a crowded
room.

- *survival.*

women
pass down
how-to guides
on the ways
to tell if
our drinks
are spiked
& offer
to guard
the flimsy doors
of bathroom stalls
for
each other.

- *survival II.*

the
only time
i know
what
being safe
feels like

is
when
i'm in
a room
overflowing
with light

& the laughter
of women
that fills
the space
floor-to-ceiling
with lavender

&
a door
with a lock
no man
can
ever break.

- *safety has never been our privilege.*

we know how to
keep the girls safe

from the
sharp talons of

old, sleepy,
bedroom-eyed dragons,

& when we aren't
quick enough to act,

we know just what
we have to do:

walk through
the roaring blaze

& swim across
miles of moats

& climb the
glittering tower

& make the beasts
beg us for our mercy.

- *predators.*

we
finally refused
to be seen as only

bodies crafted
for the men's
use&consumption,

so we set the
clouds ablaze
to sway them,

to show them
how wonderfully
we could coexist,

but
they chose to
take it as a threat

& they
have never
fully forgiven us

for claiming
the portion of the sky
that was always rightfully ours.

- *when the glass sky is the limit.*

when our abilities
became too much,

they tried to
shut us away

in the dark
without even

a candle
to guide us out.

little
did they know,

our
woman-rage-fire

would light
our path home

just fine.

- *you are your own lighthouse.*

the man with the witch-killing look in his eyes drinks deeply from the chipped lilac teacup, his trembling hands making it clink against the saucer as he places them back together. my stomach churns in circles as the dark liquid dribbles down his chin in lines. he eagerly slides the cup & dish to me across the old, rickety table & i waste no time turning the cup over onto the dish to get rid of the excess. when i turn the cup right-side up, i spot the clusters of soggy brown & black leaves that litter the bottom in various shapes & sizes. i study it for a moment & immediately look away, nervously wringing my hands in my skirts. there's no question what that means.

"well? what does it say?" he asks.

i keep my eyes down. "the leaves say you're going to . . . pay."

"p-pardon?" he sputters, his eyes filling to the brim with terror.

"they say . . . you're all going to pay," i whisper.

- *the leaves never lie.*

to be a
woman
is to be
warbound,
k n o w i n g
all the odds
are stacked
against you.

- & never giving up in spite of it.

red lipstick:
an external sign
of internal
fire.

- *we tried to warn you.*

red lipstick:
battle cry.
battle cry.
battle cry.

- *we tried to warn you II.*

they scratched it
out of the history books,

but on all the
great innovations

you will find
scorch marks

in the shape of
a woman's

magnificent
handprint.

do not forget:
we need to be
the history books
now.

- *women are libraries about to burst.*

women
don't endure
simply because
we can;

no,

women endure
because we aren't
given any other
choice.

- they wanted us weak but forced us to be strong.

they would
watch us burn

before
letting us think

we can be
our own people,

before
letting us think

we're capable
of anything

more
than they are.

- the sad, sad truth.

they
will try
to steal
your light

& use it as
a weapon
against
you.

but there's
a piece
of good
news:

they
don't have
the patience to
control it

like you do.

"you have no reason
to be afraid,"

the match-boys
tell us right before
they throw

fistfuls
& fistfuls
of matches.

"don't be so
fucking dramatic,"

the match-boys
tell us as our skin
drips into the dirt.

"you're always
overreacting,"

the match-boys
tell the reflections
in the puddles they made.

- *they only wish this is how it happened.*

always put yourself first.
sacrifice at your own
discretion.

- <u>coven rule #1.</u>

II. the burning

"the only thing we're guilty of is being women,"
we tell them,

& that's all they hear.

that's all they need to hear before they rush in
on us. that's all they need to hear before they
gather us together like cattle, adults & children
alike. that's all they need to hear before they
reveal the ropes they kept hidden behind their
backs. that's all they need to hear before they
tie us around the same old oak tree, forcing us
to hold hands with each other for comfort. ("ring
around—r-r-ring around—ring around...")

that's all they need to hear before they pick up
their feet & drag the matches across the bottoms
of their boots.

- the second lesson in fire.

to
the men,

women are
born as

delicate
rosebuds.

even
the way

they
crush us

beneath their
angry steps

leaves them
breathless.

- *wilted before the bloom.*

they
tell us
over & over
& over
again
that women
need
to stay

        small/
        thin/
        skinny/
        petite.

that way,
we are
effortlessly
pocketed
to be used
& thrown out
at a later
time.

curves
& fat
& rolls
are a
colossal
"fuck you"
to the
patriarchy—

our accidental
rebellion.

- my body rejects your desires.

she's
so scared
to
takeupspace
that even
the weight
of her
bones
sometimes
feels like
too much.

- *the hollow-girl.*

&
she
begins to
wonder
if kisses
have
calories
& how
long they
would take
to burn.

- the hollow-girl II.

I. water.
II. coffee&tea.
III. zero-calorie sweetener.
IV. one-hundred-calorie snacks.
V. a body so weightless no one else can own it.

- *a hollow-girl's grocery list.*

to
describe myself
as

        fat
        is not

to
describe myself
as

        ugly, lazy, worthless,
        or *undesirable.*

- it's my self-acceptance movement.

in our bellies:
fire fire fire
& sometimes
not much
else.

- these are the real hunger games.

in our hands:
embers embers embers
just waiting for
the opportunity
to ignite.

- catching fire is so, so easy.

the
men
make us
dance
for

them
until our
toes are
bloody
&
then
they just
tell us to
change out
our pink
slippers
for

r

e

d.

- their darling dancing dolls.

when his girlfriend
exits stage left
all the vicious villagers
gather 'round & 'round,

the *hushhushhushing*
of the dead man sea
as he takes his long-awaited leave
from the shadows

& reaches a hand out
for my blackwater hair,
rope-twisting it around
his unforgiving fist,

my neck bending back
as a white lily stem does
just before the
breath-taking & breaking.

he leans down
to kiss me with his
beautiful, blood-rusted
chainsaw mouth,

& the next morning,
all the ladies of the village
have their favorite shade of
blood splatter lip stain

named after me.

- *abuse is nothing to romanticize.*

telling me
not all men
have
bad intentions

doesn't do
anything to
reassure
me.

after i
walk away from you,
nothing will have
changed.

i will still
be scared to
leave my house
after sundown,

i will still
find comfort
in keys resting
between fingers,

i will still
question
the intentions of
every man i know,

i will still
wonder
when i am
to become

a story
meant to warn
other people's
daughters,

& i will still
cry when i turn on
the television
to find

yet
another man
getting away
with

well—
what they
always seem to
get away with.

i am not
the one who
has to change
the way i think
or the way i act.
they are.

- *expectations vs. reality.*

i hold
my tongue
out of fear
so often
that
blood
has
made
a permanent
home
in
the spaces
between
my
teeth.

- *this is what womanhood tastes like.*

we're
forced to
tread over
the still-flickering
matches
they used
to eliminate our
ancestors

&
we
still
w h i s p e r
the expected
apologies
when
our toes

get singed.

- a born regret.

a girl's first words:

"i'm sorry."
"i'm sorry."
"i'm sorry."
"i'm sorry."
"i'm sorry."
"i'm sorry."
"i'm sorry."
"i'm sorry."
"i'm sorry."
"i'm sorry."

a girl's last words:

"i'm sorry."
"i'm sorry."
"i'm sorry."
"i'm sorry."
"i'm sorry."
"i'm sorry."
"i'm sorry."
"i'm sorry."
"i'm sorry."
"i'm sorry."

they try to
convince us
that our rapists
will only ever be

strangers
lurking in bushes
in the dark,
dark night,

that we
should keep
floral pepper spray
& pocketknives

tucked
neatly into
our purses
at all times

(because
apparently
even the act
of trying not

to be raped
should look
lovely
& feminine),

so
that when
our rapists
end up being

our grandfathers/fathers/
brothers/uncles/cousins/
best friends/boyfriends/
husbands,

we have no words
to describe it
& no one willing to
help light our torches.

- everything is a distraction.

what rape culture does:

> fills me with
> fleeting relief
> when i find out that
> i escaped
> my ex-boyfriend
> before he became
> a rapist

> & not after.

- *this poison has seeped into everything.*

we spend lifetimes
combing our way
through scarce
clover fields,

hoping, praying,
finger, eye,
toe, & leg
crossing

that we're not
the 1 out of 6
who come up
empty-handed,

&
we are never
able to forgive
ourselves for being

the ones to pluck
that green amethyst hope
right before her fingers
s w e e p the thin air.

- *safety & luck hold hands with each other.*

i
can't seem
to recall
agreeing
to be a
casualty
of these
manmade
disasters.

- *cyclone.*

no one should
have to carry
the unbearably
heavy weight of
a m a t t r e s s
on their back
for a lifetime.

- for emma sulkowicz.

i'm having the nightmare again. the one where the crooked wood comes to life & the tree-man with the sharp, gnarled branches uproots himself from the soil & comes stumbling out after me. i would recognize his face anywhere. it's the face they sketched by the flow of my shaky 11-year-old words. after all these years, he finally gets to be rootless because wicked men are rarely punished for very long. his bark is dry & peeling & his exposed fruit rots from the inside out & i cannot peddle my little yellow bike away fast enough. the wheels get caught in the thick spring mud & suddenly i'm sinking & he reeks of revenge & i know nothing is stopping him this time because wicked men do not stop until they punish anyone who tries to tell them that the world isn't theirs for the taking while the wind whispers to them: "take her, take her, take her."

- *what women dream about.*

the men,
they're
d r a g g i n g
me into
the shadow forest
where not even
the wolves
dare go.

they use
my body
like men
use women's
bodies
& when they're
finally done
with me

they cut off
          my tongue
my breasts
          my hands
     my feet

& leave
no thread
behind
for me to
stitch
myself
back
together.

- *what women dream about II.*

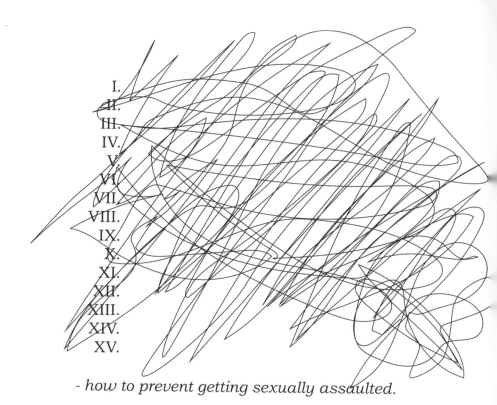

I.
II.
III.
IV.
V.
VI.
VII.
VIII.
IX.
X.
XI.
XII.
XIII.
XIV.
XV.

- how to prevent getting sexually assaulted.

I. don't rape.
II. don't rape.
III. don't rape.
IV. don't rape.
V. don't rape.
VI. don't rape.
VII. don't rape.
VIII. don't rape.
IX. don't rape.
X. don't rape.
XI. don't rape.
XII. don't rape.
XIII. don't rape.
XIV. don't rape.
XV. don't rape.

- how to prevent sexually assaulting someone.

but
what if
the devil
is just
a woman
who was
banished
to hell
to stoke
the
flames
as
punishment
for
standing up
to
him?

- *lilith.*

he
told her
not to
play
with his
poor
little
heart
so she
spared it
by walking
                    a w a y
&
that's
when he
stole
all her
smiles
& threw them
into the
dark&icy
december
waters.

- rip to the women who lost these games.

some
fathers
will

                    c r a c k
their
daughter's
teeth
with skinned
knuckles

&

when
her lover's
fist
comes
for her
she will
offer him
an open-lipped
smile.

"it's just like home,"
she'll say.

- *she didn't even have to tap her feet together.*

our
very being

is considered
an inconvenience,

our bodies
vacant homes

wrapped in layers
of yellow tape,

our legs
double doors

for one man
(& one man only)

to pry open so
he can invade us

& set down his
furniture,

never once
asking us

how we feel
about the curtains.

- *they love us empty, empty, empty.*

sometimes your demons
will be men

who show dimples
when they say "thank you"

& open doors for every
approaching stranger

& send you
good morning/good night texts

& remember
your mother's maiden name

& surprise you with good coffee
on all your bad days

& with the same voice
he uses to tell you

he loves you,
he will tell you

how he dreamed
of killing you

a dozen different ways
last night

& woke up
aching.

- *what men dream about.*

&
the men
will always sit
(too) close
to you

&
claim they
just want to
be warmed
by your
flames

&
they will
smile as
they bottle
up your
sparks

&
later they'll
tell everyone
they know how to
build such a great
& terrible fire

all by
themselves.

- women are always born on an eclipse.

they
think they
can write
our stories

because

their mothers
let them
fingertip-trace
their palms

but

their words
will always have
a distinct lack of
smoke.

*- did you really think you'd get to mourn the
house you set aflame?*

i don't need you
to write my story.

i write it
e v e r y d a y

& you couldn't
even translate

the fucking
punctuation.

- *she.*

ready for a
harsh truth?

women
don't need
your validation.

we
already have
our own.

- *my self-worth shouldn't feel like an act of bravery.*

men
so often claim
we're

mystery novels
with
collective symbolism

simultaneously
too shallow
& too difficult

for them
to ever dream of
understanding,

so instead of
taking the time to unravel
our complex plots,

they take
the easy way out—
pouring gasoline over us,

flicking
matches over
their shoulders,

&
laughing as they
walk away.

- *call us alexandria.*

following
in the
footsteps
of that
fool
icarus,

the men
were
tempted
to fingertip-graze
our impressive
flames

& had
the nerve
to be surprised
when their
manmade
wax wings

m

    e

        l

           t

              e

                  d.

- but try not to overreact, darling.

don't you know
a woman's anguish
could cause
e   x   p   l   o   s   i   o   n   s
in other
dimensions?

- if you don't, you're going to find out.

burn whoever tries to burn you.

- <u>coven rule #2.</u>

III. the firestorm

the lit matchsticks tumbletumbletumble their way towards us & stop dead just before the flames would lick hungrily at our toes. we squeeze our eyes shut, bracing ourselves for our violent end. the thick air reverberates with "i love you"s & "we will meet again"s, but the only thing that follows is silence. we reluctantly pry our eyes open when we hear the match-boys' infuriated shouting in the background.

"we would never dream of letting the match-boys use us to hurt you," the smoke murmurs soothingly to us. "shhh, don't worry. we will make them pay for this," it whispers again, wrapping its way up & around our bodies until we're consumed by a protective grey barrier.

we use our combined powers to turn the matches around.

the match-boys aren't fast enough for us.

- *the third lesson in fire.*

they can
hand us
folded dresses.

they can
gift us
virgin wings.

they can
force on us
their names.

they can
lock us in
small rooms.

they can
thieve
our words.

they can
attempt to take
our choices, too,

but the one thing
they can never
steal?

this
fierce
determination.

- *what june taught me.*

(homage to *The Handmaid's Tale* by Margaret Atwood)

society
wrapped
a corset
around us,

fisted
the strings
& pulled
tight

as if
tuning
a new
violin,

&
until we
cut them
away

&
pull out
the
bones

we will
never discover
who we
truly are.

- *unlearn this normalized self-hatred.*

we can
be skinny
& we can
be content,

but

being skinny
is not the
same thing
as being content.

- *we must come home from this everlasting battle.*

i appreciate:

    I. every roll.
    II. every scar.
    III. every acne mark.
    IV. every ~~extra~~ pound.
    V. every stretch mark.
    VI. every ~~misplaced~~ hair.
    VII. every bit of cellulite.
    VIII. the only body i have.

- things i still struggle to say & that's okay.

if
you can't
root for
yourself,

you don't
just
cut down
your tree

in order
to spite
the
ground.

no—
you breathe,
step back,
& give yourself

the
necessary
room
to flourish.

- *from the grimoire of the green witch.*

it's
more than
okay

to
wake up
with the
overwhelming urge
to cover up
all the mirrors.

self-love
is not
an instant
nor an
overnight
evolution,

but
at least try
to open up
the windows
to let the breeze in
every once in awhile.

- *a witch knows mirrors do sometimes lie.*

sip
the silky
elixir
from my
cupped
palms.

go on,
take as
much
or as little
as you
need.

let it
guide you
into a
grand
love affair
with yourself

until
the love
becomes so
second nature
you need it
no more.

here,
we'll drink together.
bottoms up.

- *self-love potion.*

you have to eat. you have to eat. you have to eat.
you have to eat. you have to eat. you have to eat.
you have to eat. you have to eat. you have to eat.
you have to eat. you have to eat. you have to eat.
you have to eat. you have to eat. you have to eat.
you have to eat. you have to eat. you have to eat.
you have to eat. you have to eat. you have to eat.
you have to eat. you have to eat. you have to eat.
you have to eat. you have to eat. you have to eat.
you have to eat. you have to eat. you have to eat.
you have to eat. you have to eat. you have to eat.
you have to eat. you have to eat. you have to eat.
you have to eat. you have to eat. you have to eat.
you have to eat. you have to eat. you have to eat.
you have to eat. you have to eat. you have to eat.
you have to eat. you have to eat. you have to eat.
you have to eat. you have to eat. you have to eat.
you have to eat. you have to eat. you have to eat.
you have to eat. you have to eat. you have to eat.
you have to eat. you have to eat. you have to eat.
you have to eat. you have to eat. you have to eat.
you have to eat. you have to eat. you have to eat.
you have to eat. you have to eat. you have to eat.
you have to eat. you have to eat. you have to eat.
you have to eat. you have to eat. you have to eat.
you have to eat. you have to eat. you have to eat.
you have to eat. you have to eat. you have to eat.
you have to eat. you have to eat. you have to eat.
you have to eat. you have to eat. you have to eat.
you have to eat. you have to eat. you have to eat.
you have to eat. you have to eat. you have to eat.
you have to eat. you have to eat. you have to eat.
you have to eat. you have to eat. you have to eat.
you have to eat. you have to eat. you have to eat.

you have to eat. you have to eat. you have to eat.
you have to eat. you have to eat. you have to eat.
you have to eat. you have to eat. you have to eat.
you have to eat. you have to eat. you have to eat.
you have to eat. you have to eat. you have to eat.
you have to eat. you have to eat. you have to eat.
you have to eat. you have to eat. you have to eat.
you have to eat. you have to eat. you have to eat.
you have to eat. you have to eat. you have to eat.
you have to eat. you have to eat. you have to eat.
you have to eat. you have to eat. you have to eat.
you have to eat. you have to eat. you have to eat.
you have to eat. you have to eat. you have to eat.
you have to eat. you have to eat. you have to eat.
you have to eat. you have to eat. you have to eat.
you have to eat. you have to eat. you have to eat.
you have to eat. you have to eat. you have to eat.
you have to eat. you have to eat. you have to eat.
you have to eat. you have to eat. you have to eat.
you have to eat. you have to eat. you have to eat.
you have to eat. you have to eat. you have to eat.
you have to eat. you have to eat. you have to eat.
you have to eat. you have to eat. you have to eat.
you have to eat. you have to eat. you have to eat.
you have to eat. you have to eat. you have to eat.
you have to eat. you have to eat. you have to eat.
you have to eat. you have to eat. you have to cat.
you have to eat. you have to eat. you have to eat.
you have to eat. you have to eat. you have to eat.
you have to eat. you have to eat. you have to eat.
you have to eat. you have to eat. you have to eat.
you have to eat. you have to eat. you have to eat.
you have to eat. you have to eat. you have to eat.
you have to eat. you have to eat. you have to eat.
you have to eat. you have to eat. you have to eat.

(homage to *Wintergirls* by Laurie Halse Anderson)

95

eat.
fill yourself
with energy,
with sunlight.
treat your body
to tenderness &
lavender.

- we need you here & whole.

i
will be
that voice
that tells you
to cover your arms
with flower petals
instead.

- your winter will come to an end.

dish:

woman

ingredients:

I. sugar
II. spite
III. everything not-so-nice

directions:

I. preheat cauldron to 375 degrees.
II. mix together ingredients in a medium
to large bowl.
III. add more spite if necessary. (& oh, will
it be necessary.)
IV. boil 10 to 12 minutes.
V. eat. have the seconds&thirds&fourths
you were always denied. lick fingers when
done.

- from the kitchen witch's cookbook.

"i don't
wear makeup for others
the same way
i don't

decorate
my house for others.
this is my
home

&
everything i do
is for
me."

- tweet from september 28th, 2016.

what
i mean
by that
is

i lost
so
many
years

of
my life
by being
too

exhausted/hunger-tired/
depressed/winter-sick
to get out
of bed—

having
no choice
but to stare endlessly
at the walls

where i ripped
the rusty
rosebud wallpaper
off

in
thin strips
with fragmented
fingernails—

to
let you believe
i only pushed myself
through the

obsessions/blood-crust/
numbers/ink-bruises
so i could
paint a

pretty little garden mural
on the door
for you & for you
alone.

- i'm not ashamed to say i'm my first priority.

quenching
his
thirst
is
not
the
point
of
this
life.

- there is so much waiting for us.

no
matter
what they
tell you,
it is
not
your job
to be
polite
to anyone
who
is not
polite
to you
first.

- get up, you are nobody's doormat.

you are

the lucky ace
of the deck,

a burning
arrow

piercing through
their so-called

hollow tree
hatred.

you. are.

- *embr(ace).*

paint
your nails
black,

rub glitter
on your
face,

take
so many
selfies,

compliment
all your
sisters

(no,
not just
your cis-ters),

& hex
any
man

who
catcalls
you.

- *a note from me scrawled on your mirror.*

"my body
is a historic city
& i'm the only one
allowed to set
the buildings
ablaze."

- reclaim yourself.

"bitch," he spits.

"witch," he sneers.

& i say,
"actually, i'm both."

- reclaim everything.

no,
women
are not
vessels
to f i l l
w i t h
y o u r
desires.

women:
unique,
original,
creative,
amazing,
human.

no copying
or pasting
can be
done
here.

- *the anti-manic pixie dream girl.*

i am not
a keepsake
you can tuck on your
bookshelf
between
your bukowski
& thoreau.

i am not
a dried daisy
you can close
in a shadowbox
& hang just
above your
sleeping head.

i am not
your kindness
participation
trophy
or anything
for you to
proudly own.

sometimes
friendship is the
motherfucking
prize,
so be grateful
i let you in
at all.

- THE FRIENDZONE DOESN'T EXIST.

script
for when
he
tells you
you're
beautiful:

"i know."

- confidence isn't egotism.

script
for when
he
tells you
to
smile:

"drop dead."

- *confidence is healthy.*

when he tells you
you would be nothing
without him,

i'll hand you
all the necessary
tools.

> *first,*
> *pour the coals*
> *down your throat.*
>
> *second,*
> *chase them down with*
> *your ready match.*

then you can
feel assured when
you tell him

he's been cleansed
from you, body
& soul,

& would you
just look at
that?

you're just fine
without
him.

- *the body regenerates whenever the hell you want.*

they don't want us
to be

mary sue's,
but

they don't want us
to be

unlikable,
either.

that begs
the question:

do they even want us
to exist

outside of their
late-night fantasies?

- i am neither your paper doll, nor your blow-up doll.

be the
	unlikable
	woman
	protagonist

(*synonyms:*
	bitch,
	realistic,
	manhero)

all the
	men
	just love to
	complain about.

- it's so much more fun that way, isn't it?

in this novel
the woman protagonist

claims she's not like
those other girls,

not because she finds
their femininity

to be an insult or
a weakness, no—

it's
because

she knows
all women have

their own unique
magic

that cannot be
replicated by her

or any other
woman.

- *the plot twist we've all been waiting for.*

there
is not
only
one
woman
body.

we are
simply
women
who happen
to have
bodies—

shelters
built to
protect our
woman-rage-fire
from
hurricanes.

- *every woman is authentic II.*

womanhood
doesn't
have to be
this twisted
competition.

let us
cultivate
womanhood
until it grows
into sisterhood.

we'll sprinkle
lavender seeds
into our
old wounds
until we're finally

h e a l e d.

- your sisters are not your enemies.

we must help lift
each other above
the flames.

- *women supporting women.*

by all means,
let your judgments
die in the blaze.

- women supporting women II.

say it
with me
now:

"i am a woman.
i am a human.
& i matter with
no conditions
attached.

you may not
see my worth,
but i do.
i do."

- *dear women.*

say it
with me
now:

"women
owe
me
nothing.

not anything.

not
one
thing."

- *dear men.*

"boys will be boys"

until the day
we raise our sons

to practice
the exact same

responsibility,
accountability,

&
maturity

we assign to our
daughters

before choosing
their names.

- *you don't teach, they don't learn.*

i'm (not) sorry
to disappoint
you,

but your
charming smirk

will no longer
excuse

the hurt you
inflict.

try
not to
flatter
yourself
by thinking
you can
ever

       b r e a k

me
when
i'm the
heroine
who had to
save
all your
favorite
childhood
superheroes.

- diana & i are on a first name basis.

call me
bitch.

call me
villain.

call me
she-wolf.

call me
bad omen.

call me
your worst nightmare

wearing a
red-lipped smile.

- even better, call me by my name.

i didn't come here
to be civil.

i didn't come here
to sit you down

with a mug of tea
& a blueberry muffin

to coddle you as
i try to convince you

that respecting
my existence is essential.

you've had plenty
of chances

& you took a
hard pass every time,

so i came here
to watch your anger overtake

until you finally
c   o   m   b   u   s   t.

- *i'll use your light to read.*

forget
being ladylike

(whatever
the hell
that means)

& allow
yourself to

show
the world
just how

unapologetically
angry

this
inequality
makes you.

let it all
                    g o.

- *throw flames like a girl.*

women,
i implore you:
build your fire.

just pretend
you're helping
the men
survive till spring
like we were
raised to.

let them get
nice & relaxed

until
their lungs
have more
smoke
than they do
air

&
no way
to call out
for
help.

dear match-boys,

you know
all those she-devils

you executed during
1692 & 1693?

well, they made sure
we inherited their power

by injecting sparks
directly into
our veins

& planting flames
at the ends of
our fingertips

& imbedding
one word at the tips of
our tongues:

"erupt."

- *katniss only wishes.*

you
gentle
(comma)
strong
(comma)
resilient
(comma)
d e a d l y
creature
(comma)
you
(period)

- you are an unstoppable force.

i'm
pretty sure
you have
                witchcraft
running
through
those
                v e i n s.

- women are some kind of magic II.

every time
you "joke" to your other
red-handed
rapist friends

that it's
not rape if
you warn them
first—

every time
you press
your callous-hard
hand

over her
pink lemonade lipstick,
"no please no"
mouth—

every time
you think of slipping
something smooth & sleepy
into her drink—

catch us
in the skies,
flying by night,
landing soundlessly behind you.

we'll
be waiting
(im)patiently with swords
pushed up our dress sleeves

&
blood-rusted spikes
sticking out of
our boots.

(oh, yes
heads will be
thump. thump. thumping.
& *r o l l i n g.)*

the knights
of the round table
kneel to
us.

arthur,
rip your
ribs wide open
& eat your heart out.

brienne,
here's our card.
we'll be waiting
for your call.

- witch girl gang.

misogyny
/mə'säjənē/
noun

1: the power-driven hatred of women.

2: just the way things are.

misandry
/mi'sandre/
noun

1: the reactionary, self-preserving hatred of men.

2: somehow this is going too far.

in my
fairy tale
version
of the story,

every
mattress
spontaneously
bursts into flames

any time
our "no"s,
any time
our silences

are met
with the
father-taught
resistance

of
hands
over mouths
& around necks

&
arms
that form
cages of steel.

the
same fire
that feeds us,
that nurtures us

never makes
bargains
with the
guilty

& we
always
walk away
uncharred.

- this is the reckoning.

according
to the news,
the woman found
her husband

touching
their daughter
with his
ice-hands,

so
as he slept
as safely
& as soundly

as
their daughter
never would
again,

the woman
considered the gun
tucked underneath
their bed,

but she decided
that bullets were
far, far too
tame

a
punishment
for what he
had done.

instead,
she got out her torch
& gave him a big
goodnight kiss.

"it's the
perfect night
for a fire,"
she remarked

to herself
as she sat back
& sipped her
wine.

- these are the new burnings.

first,

i dismembered you
like a five-year-old girl left alone

with her first plastic doll,
fascinated by the way in which

we are all so easily
taken apart

but not so easily
pieced back together.

second,

i laid your limbs out
all over my kitchen table,

ever so careful so as not to
stain the perfectly polished oak.

in the back of my mind,
i knew it would be okay even if it did;

i bleed twelve weeks a year,
so i know a thing or two about bloodstains.

(your messed up, mangled limbs
felt colder to the touch than the icicle words

you dropped down on my head
that last night.)

finally,

i buried some of your parts
in the garden where only green things grow;

i buried some of your parts
in the spider-webbed walls

of the abandoned attic;
i burned some of your parts—

your smoke cursing
the silver lightning sky—

before sprinkling your ashes
over the sickening sea.

(i don't consider myself
a spidery, spiteful, spitfire woman,

but if i'm never going to be whole again,
then neither are you.)

- how i got over you.

she
wished for

him to burn
& oh, how that

motherfucker
burned

&

oh, how
exquisite the

new life was that
she built from his

blackened
bones.

- no longer helpless.

(homage to the musical *Hamilton* by Lin-Manuel Miranda)

gather 'round, gather 'round.

are you comfortable?

very good. because this poem goes out to all the match-boys who mistakenly considered me to be a silly little girl unworthy of their truth, unworthy of their love, & unworthy of their respect. know that every time you jerk awake mid-freefall, it was me who pushed you out of your 3 A.M. dreams. & know that whenever you feel that chill creeping up & down your spine on a warm summer's day, i'm the one who's been dancing all over your grave. & know that whenever you think you spot a shadow in your peripheral, it's just me, making sure you never hurt another woman again.

it's such a shame that you will finally have to learn that there are consequences to treating women like they're *n o t h i n g.*

you may have gotten to walk away, but a piece of me will follow you forever.

now, isn't that romantic?

- vengeance is the new moving on.

maybe
i'm not the
"crazy ex-girlfriend."

maybe
i'm just a person
reacting rationally

to the abuse
& disregard
for women

that
society has
somehow

convinced us
is completely
normal.

- *i refuse to pretend anymore.*

do you hate me yet?
do you hate me yet?
do you hate me yet?
do you hate me yet?
do you hate me yet?
do you hate me yet?
do you hate me yet?
do you hate me yet?
do you hate me yet?
do you hate me yet?
do you hate me yet?
do you hate me yet?
do you hate me yet?
do you hate me yet?
do you hate me yet?
do you hate me yet?
do you hate me yet?
do you hate me yet?
do you hate me yet?
do you hate me yet?
do you hate me yet?
do you hate me yet?
do you hate me yet?
do you hate me yet?
do you hate me yet?
do you hate me yet?
do you hate me yet?
do you hate me yet?
do you hate me yet?
do you hate me yet?
do you hate me yet?
do you hate me yet?
do you hate me yet?

if
the very
idea
of
standing up
for myself
frightens you
so
damn much
then
i guess
the power
you thought
you held
over me
wasn't that
impressive
in the
first place.

- *fragile masculinity.*

but
i digress.

what i've been
trying to say

this whole time
is that

when you
wrong me

you'll be
expecting me to

forgive you
like a

good, well-mannered
woman,

when in actuality
you'll finally

get to know
what fire tastes like.

- & no, it won't be like whiskey.

make no apologies; accept no apologies.

- <u>coven rule #3.</u>

IV. the ashes

there's the whole story as it was told to me. the witches took the flames meant to eradicate them & turned them back on their killers instead. can you believe they ever thought they would get away with it? i know, i know. now i pass a handful of the sparks to you, daring one. show them the same mercy they showed our ancestors all those years ago. (none, none, none.) let us write their story in the ashes of their enemies, & then we can finally finish what they started.

if nothing else, we will make certain they'll never be granted the opportunity to silence us again.

don't be scared. even if you don't believe in your-self, i believe. i've always believed in you.

you know just what to do.

- *the last lesson in fire.*

they
said
poetry
was dead,
so
the tired
but
ever-determined
women
took that
as a
challenge
&
came together
to cast
their
resurrection
spell.

- necromancers.

i'm a poet
& i do
fucking
know it.

sit up
&
pay
attention

as
i take
your
name

& drag it
through
the very
flames

you
built with
my ruination
in mind.

- *i won't repeat myself.*

i have to warn you, my love. the men will try to convince you that we stole the poetry from them. they will light those stubby matches & try to throw them at us once more, but they will miss & they will not be happy. oh no, not. one. bit. "give it back!" they'll shout at us until their throats start to bleed. they mean give it back to the dead men who thought they were taking the poetry with them to the grave, the same dead men who were so naïve as to think that the words wouldn't slip from their grip after their skin decomposed & their marrow began to show. the irony? it was our men who demanded we go outside to tend to their sunflowers, never once dreaming of the possibility that we would wander away into their cemeteries.

- *finders keepers.*

unzip
the skin
around all
my edges

&
you will find
the grave-robbed
bones

of all
the women poets
wronged by
men

they
would
never dare
satisfy by dying.

they
continue to write
through my
hand

& a woman's
wrath
is nothing
if not immortal.

- *writing with no light.*

i know
about
that voice
inside
you.

yes,
i know
all about
the
woman

who's
been
screaming
her whole
life

for
the chance
to be
heard
by someone.

take
this pen
from me
& uncage
                    her.

- *you owe this to yourself.*

you
think
your body
is made up
of mostly
water,

but
really
your body
is made up
of mostly
poetry.

wherever you go,
you leave behind
puddles of
words
in your
wake.

collect the
integral pieces
of yourself
&
call the
words back.

you deserve
to be whole again.

- *the sign you've been waiting for II.*

we need
your words.

we need
your experiences,

we need
your traumas,

we need
your anger,

we need
your guilt,

we need
your passions,

we need
the story

you think no one
cares to hear.

we need that
woman-rage-fire

only you
can provide, so

write.
write.
write.

- *the sign you've been waiting for III.*

write the poem.
(write the pain)
burn the poem.
(burn the pain)

- blow the ashes in their eyes.

poetry
will be
the thing
that
leads us
into this
revolution

&

poetry
will be
the thing
that
leads us
carefully
back out.

- resistance is fine art.

silence → ilence → iolence →
violence

protest → potest → poetst →
poett → poetr →
poetry

two hands
cupped around
the earth,
cracked open
the middle,
& poured its
contents
into a
black hole.

no light—
only the
soundless,
suffocating
dark
with no
escape.

that
is the
only way
i know how to
describe

~~the agony.~~

- ~~1/20/17~~

when you
take it upon
yourself
to politicize
human bodies
&
the
right to
keep breathing
without paying
a steep price
for it,
don't
pretend
to be shocked
when we start
to take politics
personally.

- as you tell us, "deal with it."

january 21st, 2017.
remember the date.

it was the day when more
than 3.3 million women

took the flames
that have licked at

their hard&soft skin
for centuries

& threw barrels of it
at the old house

constructed with packs of
white matchsticks.

- *the women's marches.*

in response,
the match-boys

locked all the windows
& all the doors

to silence us, which only meant
we had to scream louder.

oh, how the sky fell&fell
for days afterward—

some believe they were
the tears of the ancestors

who had to watch but couldn't
stop this from happening.

- *the women's marches II.*

&
when it
was all over,
we gathered
together
& raised
our faces—
eyes closed—
towards
the sky.

a cry/a plead/
a thanks
to the woman
who fought to
keep our fire
alive
but got
pushed into
the pit
instead.

thank you
for believing
we could be
more than
fading embers.

- for hillary.

fight tirelessly
for your sisters

& don't forget
to lend a hand to

those pushed so far
into the margin

of the paper
they're   d
              a
              n
              g
              l
              i
              n
              g

off the
edge.

- *there's plenty of room for all of us.*

fire
was
made
to
bring
down
walls.

- he will try to divide us.

walls
should
only
be built
to keep out
flammable
tyrants.

- & we will ensure that he fails.

a
heavy crown
spray-painted gold
will still crack
when it takes
the long
tumble

d
o
w
n,

d
o
w
n,

d
o
w
n.

- the crooked king.

there will be nothing
for them to rule
if we

turn this kingdom
upside
down.

- *demolition.*

fuck
the idea of
staying calm.

there's no
such thing as a
kind uprising.

there are
no "please"s,
no "thank you"s,

&
no justice
without yelling.

- *patience is a virtue we can't afford.*

fat
women,
old women,
poor women,
trans women,
queer women,
jewish women,
women of color,
muslim women,
disabled women,
indigenous women,
mentally ill women,
chronically ill women,
neurodivergent women,
& all the people in
all the margins
of this page.

together & only together
shall we finally

RISE. RISE.
RISE. RISE.
RISE. RISE.
RISE. RISE.
RISE. RISE.
RISE. RISE.
RISE. RISE.
RISE. RISE.
RISE. RISE.
RISE.

- *no one will be left in dark, dusty corners.*

point your
red gold palms
towards the
kingdom.

melt it.
        melt it.
                melt it.

resurrect
a queendom
in its
place—

a protected
sanctuary where
we can finally
be equal.

don't
you dare
wait for
permission.

that's never
gotten us
anywhere,
has it?

- *they had their turn.*

here's
the tricky thing
about fire:

it stays soft
even while it
destroys

everything
in its
path,

but
it's up
to you

to
make sure
that

it doesn't
burn the
good

with
the rot.

- *we can't lose our empathy.*

in the
dark den of the
witch-queens'
castle

we celebrate
a war won.

blood orange juices
dribble down
our
chins&necks,

caught by
tasting tongues.

strawberries
stain
our fingers
down to the knuckle,

cleaned by
moaning mouths.

raspberries
get tangled up
in our
braided hair,

picked out with
teasing teeth.

&
half-nibbled pluots
plop into
our laps,

       retrieved by
       first-time fingers.

- she loved the feast.

(homage to the poem "Goblin Market" by Christina Rossetti)

don't let anyone
make you believe

it's not okay
for you to be angry

when you're mistreated
time & time again,

but what happens
the next morning

when you go to
the window

to let the sun
warm your face

& you catch a glimpse
of the way the rays

reflect off the world
you intended to fix

but made
wreckage of

instead?

- we must be better than them.

when
this war ends
at last,

follow me
back out
into

the
quiet of the
day,

&
with your
tired palms

scoop up
a pile of the
rubble,

mourn it as it
falls through
your fingers,

& then
keep going.
there's much work to do.

- *reconstruction.*

queens
do not need
to curtsy before
anyone.

queens
do not need
delicate kisses on
the back of their hands.

queens
do not need
to apologize before
making demands.

queens
do not need
to ask for anyone's
approval.

&
in this castle
made of
witch-fire
we are all
motherfucking
queens.

- & *they drank wine & laughed forever & ever.*

as
a queen,

you have
two choices:

you can
be malevolent

& ensure
our end,

or

you can be
benevolent

& love
this world

back
to life.

- a new chapter awaits, witch-queens.

didn't
you know
there
could be

        shelves
        upon
        shelves
        upon
        shelves
        of books

written
about
your
strength?

- as always, the women save themselves in this one.

know that anger has its limits
& act accordingly.

- <u>coven rule #4</u>

& silence.

today
you are
the fire

& tomorrow
you will be
the sea

& they'll
have no choice
but to hear your siren song.

- amanda lovelace

⌛

until
next time:
shine so brightly
the men think you're
guiding them into
the afterlife.

- you are invincible.

special acknowledgments

I. *cyrus parker* – thank you for staying patient with me while the writing process of this book tore me apart for months. i'll never be able to fully express my gratitude for all that you've done for me over the years. you truthfully are the better half of me, my poet-husband. <3

II. *christine day* – bambi, my best friend, my writing cheerleader, & my sister-soul mate . . . endless thank you's for reading each & every draft of this collection & for convincing me that this story was something worth telling, even when it was the slushiest of slush piles. i wouldn't be a writer without you.

III. *my family* – my sisters, my dad, my stepmom, & all the rest. i was terrified you wouldn't support my first poetry collection because of how many demons i worked through for all to witness. i'm so relieved you proved my irrational fears wrong. it's because of your endless pride for accomplish-ments that i felt confident enough to continue my writing journey.

IV. *aaron kent* – thank you for writing the prompt that inspired "prophecy I," which in turn inspired this whole collection. (this poem was originally written for & appeared first on aaron's poetry project site, poetic interviews [*poeticinterviews.wordpress.com*]. it is included in this collection with permission.)

V. *my beta readers* – mira, danika, shauna, megan, liv, mason, summer, & trista. i wouldn't have felt comfortable putting this book out into the world had it not been in your hands first. thank you, thank you, thank you for taking care of my tiny fiery witch child.

VI. *my fellow poetesses* – thank you for welcoming me so warmly into this beautiful community of women poets. the constant outpouring of support you provide was essential to the completion of this collection.

VII. *patty rice* – you're the best editor a girl could ask for. somehow you managed to change my life with a single e-mail. thank you for the love you've shown for my words & everything you've done to further my dreams.

VIII. *my readers* – this is for you. i didn't do this, *we* did this. i can't wait to see what art you put out into the world. never stop creating. we need it now more than ever.

write yourself in:

_____

about the author

growing up a word-devourer & avid fairy tale lover, it was only natural that amanda lovelace began writing books of her own, & so she did. when she isn't reading or writing, she can be found waiting for pumpkin spice coffee to come back into season & binge-watching *gilmore girls*. (before you ask: team jess all the way.) the life-long poetess & storyteller currently lives in new jersey with her fiancé, their moody cat, & a combined book collection so large it will soon need its own home. she has her B.A. in english literature with a minor in sociology. her first collection, *the princess saves herself in this one*, won the goodreads choice award for best poetry of 2016. this is her second poetry collection.

Andrews McMeel Publishing
a division of Andrews McMeel Universal
1130 Walnut Street, Kansas City, Missouri 64106

www.andrewsmcmeel.com

ISBN: 978-1-4494-8942-7

Library of Congress Control Number: 2017956019

Editor: Patty Rice
Designer: Amanda Lovelace
Art Director: Julie Barnes
Production Editor: David Shaw
Production Manager: Cliff Koehler